GOD LOVES ME TOO !

By: Charity Publications International, Inc.
Written By: Raven Malone
Illustrated By: Carlos Gonzalez
Computer Graphics: Nina Cooper
Edited By: Darrell Cameron

Bible References

Noah— Genesis chapters 5:9 through 9:29
Joseph— Genesis chapters 37, 39 through 48
Moses—Exodus chapters 2 through 40
David—I Samuel chapters 16&17. The story of David's life continues through I & II Samuel and in I Kings chapter 2:12. David also wrote many of the Psalms.
Job—The book of Job.
Shadrach, Meshach, and Abed-Nego—Daniel Chapters 2:46 through 3:30
Daniel—The book of Daniel.
Jesus—the books of Matthew, Mark, Luke, and John. The story of Jesus continues in the New Testament through the book of Revelation.
Saul/Paul—Acts chapters 8:1 and 3; 9:1-30. From Acts 13:9 on, Saul is called Paul the apostle and is the writer of much of the New Testament.

To all the good people who made this book possible, we offer a special Thank You.

ONLY THOSE WHO SEE THE INVISIBLE CAN DO THE IMPOSSIBLE!
II Cor. 4:18

To the Parents...
or Guardians

All of us at Charity Publications would like to thank you for choosing ***God Loves Me Too!*** as a means to teach your children the word of God. We would also like to encourage you to read to your children the rest of these stories from the Bible (see references).

Our book is no substitute for God's word. However, what Willie does in this book is point out that God uses all types of people. Willie also shows that we are all a little different, but with God we are all the same.

So, as you and your children read this book and the Bible references, please take note of the lessons within the lesson.

Noah has to be pure of heart, faithful, and obedient to God. It is because of Noah's obedience to God that his family and the animals are saved from the flood.
The Bible tells our children just how important obedience is. (Read Eph. 6: 1-4)
Joseph proves that when God is for you it doesn't matter who is against you.
Also, what is meant for evil, God can turn to good.
Moses is impaired by his lack of speaking ability, but God uses him in a great way.
David teaches us complete trust in God and that with God's help we can win any battle.
Job shows that nothing in this life that the enemy (the Devil) throws at us should stop us.
Have faith in God and you will pass every test.
Shadrach, Meshach, Abed-Nego, and Daniel demonstrate their uncompromised faith in God. These men have to trust God for their lives.

Of course, there is ***Jesus***, our teacher, healer, savior, who while on earth gave us all He had.

Paul is first known as mean old Saul. But it's from this man we learn the value of Repentance. By simply repenting of his past sins, Paul is used by God in a mighty way. He goes on to write nearly two-thirds of the New Testament.

Then, in the end, ***Willie*** shows us our ultimate prize for our faithfulness, obedience, and our steadfast trust in God.

It is our goal at Charity Publications to help make a difference in the lives of children everywhere. By giving you the parent, guardian, or teacher another tool to use, we can help make that difference. By using ***Wheeling Willie***, a child who is physically challenged, we make the point that all children are precious to God. So, regardless of our differences; it's God who can make the difference in all of our lives.

Wheeling Willie - God Loves Me Too!

Hey, it's me Willie! As you can see,
I do things a little differently.

Like most kids I dream of a room full of toys,
but its my Bible that brings me joy.

So, I look at the Bible and read an old story and think of God in all His glory.

So, when other kids treat me differently…
I know I'm in real good company.

First there was Noah, a man who pleased God with the purist of heart. Then one day God told him to build a great big Ark.

When Noah finished this boat, so proudly he stood, looking at his Ark of Gopher wood. All the while people made fun of him, but when it started raining, they all wanted in!

Joseph was a special boy with a coat of many colors: his problem came from his jealous brothers. So when they threw him in a hole, he prayed, "God deliver my soul."

11

Well, God gave him a hand, he was sold to a passing caravan. Even though it broke his heart, Joseph went to Egypt for a brand new start.

Years later, when Joseph's brothers came to Egypt needing food; it was *Governor Joseph* they met in fear. But, he welcomed them with love and a joyous cheer.

Pharaoh's daughter saved Moses from his tiny basket on the river. She had no idea one day God's people he'd deliver.

God had to put on quite a show before Pharaoh would let his people go. But, Moses could not say the words, so it was Aaron's voice the Pharaoh heard…"Let My People Go."

16

As the children of Israel made their way to freedom, the Red Sea had to part. God told Moses, "Just hold out your staff and I'll do my part!"

When Moses went to the mountain
to talk to God about everyone's soul,
the people made an idol of gold.

Then came one of the greatest Bible acts when down from the mountain the TEN COMMANDMENTS he brought back.

David was always on the alert to keep his father's sheep from being hurt. But, it was playing his harp that gave him joy; he was such a good boy.

"I'll fight Goliath," but in Saul's armor David was a funny sight and said, "In this armor I can not fight! But, five stones and my sling will work just right."

When we look at this deed of a boy alone,
we know it was God who guided that stone...

Then that giant fell like a ton.
That's when all Israel knew God's victory was won.

Esther had no father or mother, but God would raise her up like no other. The Bible tells how she became Queen Esther.

As Queen, Esther was living a dream. Later she would risk it all, even her life, to save her people from an evil scheme.

Job was a man whose faith never grew cold. The devil could take anything but Job's life he was told; God knew Job's faith would hold…

...Even when Job lost everything and was begging at the gate, God, he could never hate.

So, Job's life had a great ending. God blessed him with more than he had in the beginning.

WOW!
What's going to happen next?

Shadrach, Meshach, and Abed-Nego were young men who were full of glee, but they refused to bow down to the King's idol, you see.

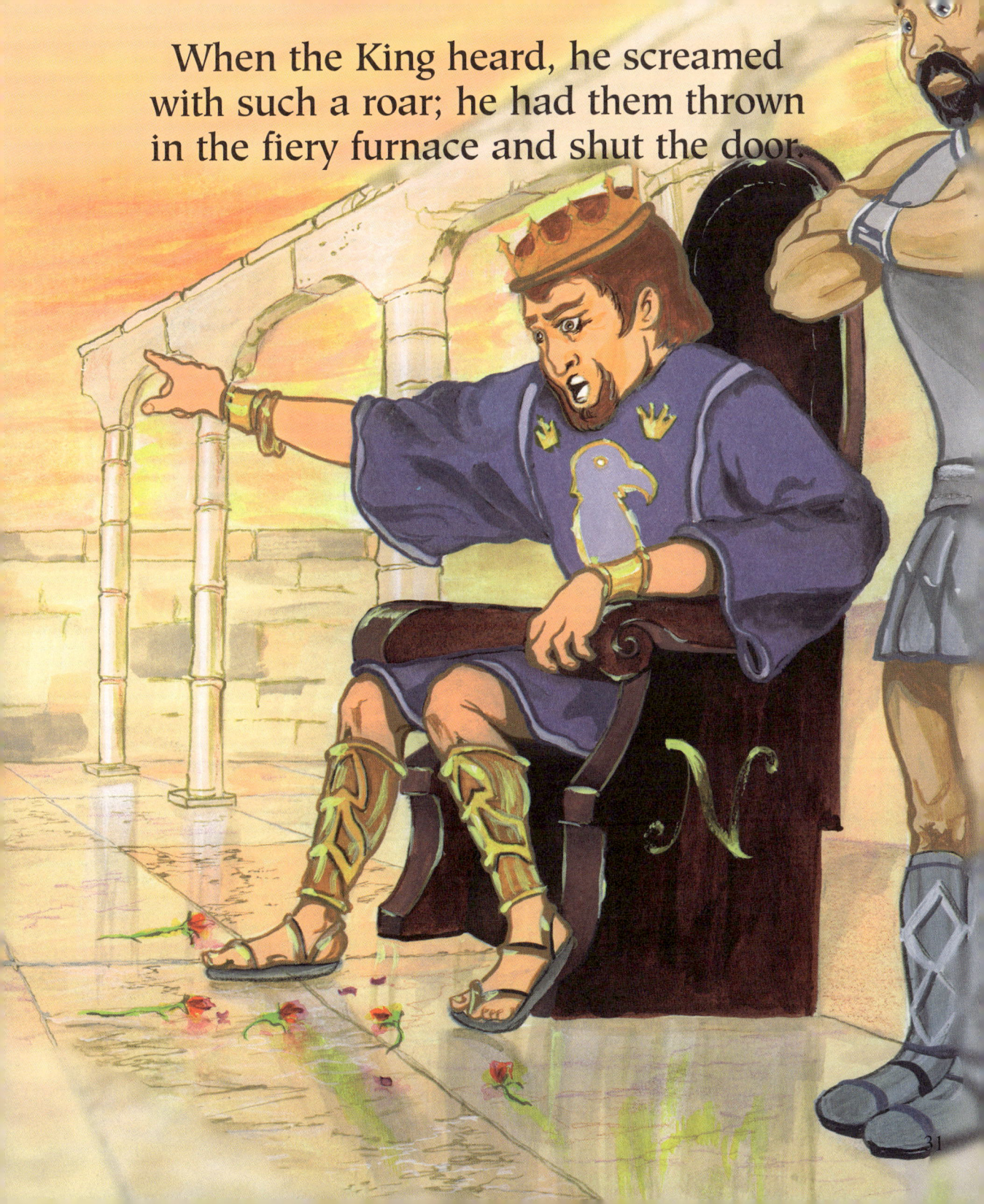

When the King heard, he screamed with such a roar; he had them thrown in the fiery furnace and shut the door.

But in the furnace to everyone's surprise, instead of three men there were four. And who was that fourth man? The Bible said it looked like the "Son of God!"

Everyone thought that Daniel's life would end when he was tossed in the lions' den.

But when morning came, Daniel said, "There's no cause for alarm; God has kept me from harm."

Jesus was a beautiful baby lying in his manger, but soon his own people would treat him like a stranger.

Later, God's word He would spread and one day five thousand He fed. This was done with five loaves and two fishes. This was a miracle, not wishes.

But, for you and me He paid the price as on the cross He gave his life. Not for just those of wealth and fame, He also died for the sick and the lame.

The way Saul treated God's
people was nothing but wrong,
so to this man we'll say, "So long!"

Then, Saul was blinded by a light from heaven and took a fall. God said, "You will no longer be known as Saul; from now on your name is Paul."

Later, the apostle Paul would work into the night as most of the New Testament he would write.

Each of these people did things a little differently, but always with God. I know I'm in good company.

Remember this, "Jesus loves the little children, All the children of the world. Red and yellow, black and white"-- no matter how different -- "we are precious in his sight..." He loves us All.

Blessed are the children for they will inherit the Kingdom of God.

So, when Jesus comes back, this life will be over and I'm going to Heaven. Because everyone knows…
GOD LOVES ME TOO!

"Welcome to Heaven, WALKING WILLIE!"

Testimonial

As a retired college professor in early seventies and recovering from two separate, serious cancers, I have had to rethink my future in terms of priorities. **Wheeling Willie** (as I review the series of manuscripts) has become an inspirational lesson to me in his determination and optimism in the face of adversity, even at his young age! Truly, I have come to believe, like *Willie*, **GOD LOVES ME TOO!**

Willie has also provided for me in retrospect an even greater understanding and appreciation for those among my students who were physically challenged. I always thought I had related to them well, for they were **Dedicated Achievers** and an absolute delight to teach. Today, I realize also they were all simply grown up versions of **Wheeling Willie.**

Jacques A. Brown

The story of **Wheeling Willie** became an instant favorite of my young students as soon as I shared it with them. What appeared to them at first to be a typical little book about a typical little boy soon became a story near and dear to their hearts. I love to watch the faces of my students every time we read the story again. I see their fascination with the exquisite and colorful illustrations, their attentiveness to the simple yet moving text and their compassion for **Willie** and for the others who share a similar situation in life. I highly recommend this book for any classroom or library. It provides a look at a side of human life that we just may be overlooking.

Sandra Waldron

Wheeling Willie is a must for every elementary school student. What a wonderful way to expose children to the world of physically challenged people. **Willie** teaches children to look beyond the outward appearances and accept others for what is within.

Debbie Radford

"Welcome to Heaven, **WALKING WILLIE!**"

Testimonial

As a retired college professor in early seventies and recovering from two separate, serious cancers, I have had to rethink my future in terms of priorities. ***Wheeling Willie*** (as I review the series of manuscripts) has become an inspirational lesson to me in his determination and optimism in the face of adversity, even at his young age! Truly, I have come to believe, like ***Willi****e*, **GOD LOVES ME TOO!**

Willie has also provided for me in retrospect an even greater understanding and appreciation for those among my students who were physically challenged. I always thought I had related to them well, for they were **Dedicated Achievers** and an absolute delight to teach. Today, I realize also they were all simply grown up versions of ***Wheeling Willie.***

Jacques A. Brown

The story of ***Wheeling Willie*** became an instant favorite of my young students as soon as I shared it with them. What appeared to them at first to be a typical little book about a typical little boy soon became a story near and dear to their hearts. I love to watch the faces of my students every time we read the story again. I see their fascination with the exquisite and colorful illustrations, their attentiveness to the simple yet moving text and their compassion for ***Willie*** and for the others who share a similar situation in life. I highly recommend this book for any classroom or library. It provides a look at a side of human life that we just may be overlooking.

Sandra Waldron

Wheeling Willie is a must for every elementary school student. What a wonderful way to expose children to the world of physically challenged people. ***Willie*** teaches children to look beyond the outward appearances and accept others for what is within.

Debbie Radford